PHYSICAL SCIENCE IN DEPTH

MAGNETS AND ELECTROMAGNETISM

Alfred J. Smuskiewicz and Tony Imbimbo

Heinemann Library
Chicago, Illinois

Customer Service 888-454-2279
Visit our website at www.heinemannlibrary.com

Produced for Heinemann Library by White-Thomson Publishing Ltd.
Illustrations: Kerry Flaherty and Q2A Solutions
Photo Research: Amy Sparks
Production: Duncan Gilbert
Originated by Modern Age Repro
Printed and bound in China by South China Printing Company Ltd.

12 11 10 09 08
10 9 8 7 6 5 4 3 2 1

Library of Congress Cataloging-in-Publication Data
Smuskiewicz, Alfred J.
  Magnets and electromagnetism / Alfred J. Smuskiewicz and Tony Imbimbo.
     p. cm. — (Physical science in depth)
  Includes bibliographical references and index.
  ISBN 978-1-4034-9927-1 (library binding - hardcover)
  ISBN 978-1-4034-9935-6 (pbk.)
 1. Magnets—Juvenile literature. 2. Magnetic fields—Juvenile literature.
3. Electromagnetism—Juvenile literature. I. Title.
  QC757.5.S68 2008
  538—dc22   2007006272

Acknowledgments
The authors and publishers are grateful to the following for permission to reproduce copyright material: Alamy **title page** and **p. 31** (Phototake Inc.); Corbis **pp. 18** (Kevin Fleming), **22** (Colin Anderson/ Brand X), **32** (Mark Ralston/Reuters), **48** (Clouds Hill Imaging Ltd.), **51** (Stephanie Maze), **52**, **53** (Reuters), **54** (STScI/NASA), **56** (NASA/epa); Getty Images **pp. 5** (Shannon Fagan/ Photonica), **9** (Visuals Unlimited), **45** (Lester Lefkowitz), **46** (Harry Sieplinga/HMS Images); iStockphoto.com **pp. 10** (Matthew Cole), **11** (Bill Noll), **14** (Ina Peters), **15** (Bryan Busovicki), **17** (Roman Krochuk), **37** (Lawrence Sawyer), **39** (George Argyropoulos), **41** (Sean Bolt); NASA **pp. 36** (ESA/J. Hester and A. Loll, Arizona State Univ.), **43**, **50**, **59** (ESA/S. Beckwith, STScI/the HUDF Team); Photolibrary/Phototake Inc. **p. 7**; Science Photo Library **pp. 20** (Jeremy Walker), **24** (Aleksander Krol), **28** (Lora Clark), **40** (Tony McConnell), **47** (Cordelia Molloy), **49** (David Parker), **57** (Lynette Cook)

Cover photograph of iron filings showing the magnetic field surrounding a bar magnet is reproduced with permission of Photolibrary/Phototake Inc.

Every effort has been made to contact copyright holders of any material reproduced in this book. Any omissions will be rectified in subsequent printings if notice is given to the publisher.

The publishers would like to thank Ann and Patrick Fullick, Timothy Griffin, and Barbara Bakowski for their assistance in the preparation of this book.

Contents

Words printed in the text in bold, **like this**,
are explained in the Glossary.

The Magic of Magnets

Magnets come in all shapes and sizes, and they work in all kinds of devices. They can be tiny enough to fit in cell phones and CD players and powerful enough to lift cars and transport high-speed trains.

People use magnets every day. Magnets hold notes to refrigerator doors—and they keep the door itself tightly closed. A magnet connected to an electric wire makes a doorbell ring. Small magnets embedded in a computer store all your software and files. Because Earth itself is a giant magnet with north and south poles, compasses with magnets can guide us around the world.

What is a magnet? It is an object that attracts or repels certain kinds of metals, including iron, steel, cobalt, and nickel. A magnet has an invisible force called **magnetism**, and this force creates a **magnetic field** around the magnet. The magnetic field is an invisible area where the magnet's force can be felt. Magnetic fields vary in size and strength. A simple bar magnet (a rectangular magnet with its north and south poles at opposite ends) might have a magnetic field extending several inches, while the magnetic field of Earth is huge—it surrounds the entire planet.

Did you know...?

Picking up a bar magnet from a table is a lot easier than pulling a magnet from a refrigerator door. Why? Because the force of magnetism is much more powerful than **gravity**—the force that keeps our feet on the ground and that causes objects to fall. In fact, the gravitational pull of our planet is not even strong enough to prevent a small refrigerator magnet from lifting a paper clip off the ground.

MAGNETISM AND ELECTRICITY

In the 1800s, scientists learned that they could turn a copper wire into a magnet by running an electric current through it. It may not seem obvious that magnetism and electricity have much in common, but they do. In fact, magnetism is caused by the motion of **electrons**, tiny particles with negative electric charges. Electrons move around the **nucleus**, or center, of an **atom**. An atom is the smallest unit of matter. When electricity and magnetism combine, they make up a force called **electromagnetism**. Electromagnetism is one of the four fundamental forces at work in the universe.

Because electric currents can be switched on and off, so too can **electromagnets**. This property makes electromagnets useful in all sorts of electrical devices, including hair dryers, remote controls, telephones, and electric motors. Magnets and electromagnetism also play an important role in many medical techniques and in such scientific quests as understanding Earth's history and exploring other planets.

You can learn much about magnetism right in your home—and you might be surprised where your investigations lead. The study can take you from your favorite refrigerator magnet to the distant stars of the universe!

A magnet's invisible magnetic field can penetrate paper, plastic, and other kinds of materials. This makes magnets perfect for hanging photos on a refrigerator door.

Magnetic Fields and Magnetic Poles

If you slide a magnet near a paper clip, there comes a point at which the paper clip will jump toward the magnet. The distance the paper clip travels to reach the magnet gives an indication of the size of the magnetic field around the magnet.

Magnetic fields are invisible. Yet scientists know about them because of the way magnets attract or repel objects that come near them. Scientists often describe magnetic fields by referring to their **magnetic poles** and **magnetic lines of force**.

MAGNETIC POLES

You have probably noticed that when you bring two magnets together, they either attract or repel each other. This reaction is due to their magnetic poles. All magnets have two poles, a north pole and a south pole. The poles are on opposite ends of the magnet. No matter what shape the magnet takes—whether it is a horseshoe, bar, or disk—the magnet will always have two poles. Opposite poles (north-south) attract each other, and like poles (north-north and south-south) repel.

Did you know...?

If you cut a magnet in half, each half of the magnet would still have a north pole and a south pole. No matter how many times you chopped up the magnet, its poles would remain intact. You would simply have smaller magnets.

MAGNETIC LINES OF FORCE

A magnetic field consists of magnetic lines of force that flow in a loop around the magnet. These lines, also known as magnetic field lines, travel out from the north pole of the magnet, curve around the sides of the magnet, and re-enter the magnet at its south pole. The strength of the magnetic field is strongest at the poles, where the lines of force are closest together.

Scientists use a unit called a **tesla** or another unit called a **gauss** to measure the strength of a magnetic field. One tesla equals 10,000 gauss. The strength of the magnetic field of a refrigerator magnet is about 0.01 tesla, or 100 gauss. An electromagnet of between 1 and 2 tesla is capable of lifting a high-speed train. Some powerful laboratory magnets produce magnetic fields with strengths of more than 30 tesla.

We can see the magnetic lines of force around two bar magnets by placing glass over the magnets and sprinkling iron filings on top of the glass. Notice how the filings loop from the north pole to the south pole of each magnet and how the filings near the north poles move away from (repel) each other.

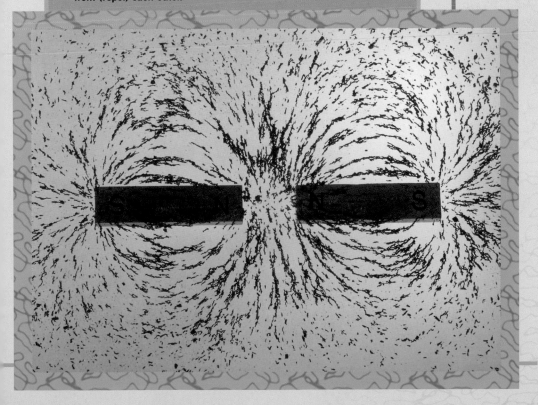

HOW MAGNETISM HAPPENS

Magnetism is caused by the movement of electrons in atoms. As an electron **orbits** the nucleus of an atom, it also spins like a top. This spinning creates a tiny magnetic field with north and south poles. In most atoms, one electron is paired up with another electron that is spinning in the opposite direction, and their magnetic fields cancel each other out.

Some atoms, however, have more electrons spinning one way than the other. When such atoms group together in one area, they create a **magnetic domain**. The magnetic fields of all the atoms in a magnetic domain are aligned. Their north poles all face one direction, and their south poles all face the opposite direction. So each domain is like a tiny magnet with a north and south pole.

Electrons that orbit an atom can spin either left to right or right to left. Here, the electrons are paired (an equal number of them are spinning in both directions), so their magnetic fields cancel each other out.

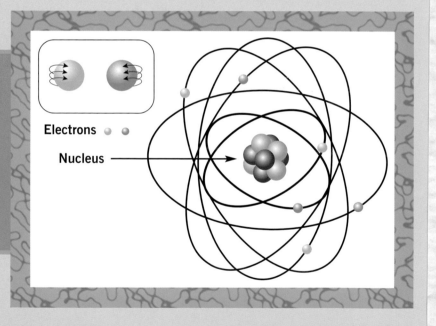

Electrons

Nucleus

There are many domains in a single material. In most materials, the domains are arranged randomly, so their poles point in all different directions. The domains cancel each other out, and they do not create a magnetic field. In a magnet, however, nearly all the domains are aligned. The combined force of the aligned domains gives the material a magnetic field.

CASE STUDY Lodestone Shows the Way

People in ancient Greece and China wrote about the magnetic properties of lodestone, a dark rock made of a mineral called **magnetite**. In ancient China, the rock was called *tzhu shih*, or "loving stone," because it was said to kiss other rocks. The Chinese noticed that when a chunk of lodestone was allowed to rotate freely, it would point in a north-south direction. Chinese engineers used this property of lodestone to help them align buildings in the directions that they wanted. The Chinese also developed the first compasslike device—a spoon made of lodestone balanced on a brass plate so that the handle of the spoon could rotate south.

In ancient Greece, a legend arose about a shepherd named Magnes, who noticed that iron nails in his boots and the iron tip of his staff stuck to the black rock. The rock was discovered in the town of Magnesia, from which the name *magnetite* is derived. The Greeks also called the rock "the stone of Heraclea," after their legendary hero Heracles. In the early 1500s, Europeans named the rock lodestone, referring to its use in compasses. *Lodestone* is derived from "leading stone," or guiding stone.

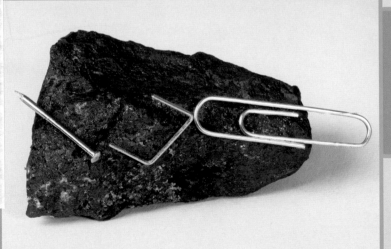

Lodestone is nature's magnet. Lodestone is made mostly of magnetite, a mineral consisting of iron and oxygen. Rocks like this one were once brought aboard ships to magnetize compass needles.

TYPES OF MAGNETS

There are three main types of magnets: **temporary magnets**, **permanent magnets**, and electromagnets. Each type of magnet has special properties that make it useful for a variety of applications.

TEMPORARY MAGNETS

When a magnet touches a steel nail, the nail itself becomes a magnet—it can pick up other nails. But when the magnet and the nail are separated, the nail loses its magnetism.

The steel nail is an example of a temporary magnet. The magnetic domains in a normal steel nail have random alignments. When the nail touches the magnet, the magnetic force of the magnet causes the magnetic domains inside the nail to align in a north-south direction and create a magnetic field. When the magnet is removed, the magnetic domains inside the nail return to their original random alignment. The nail is no longer magnetic.

Temporary magnets are made of "soft" magnetic materials, such as iron. These materials gain and lose their magnetism easily. As a result, they are useful in devices in which changing magnetic fields are necessary, such as electric motors.

Some temporary magnets can be made into permanent magnets. Repeatedly stroking an iron needle in the same direction with a magnet causes the magnetic domains in the needle to align permanently. As a result, the needle becomes a permanent magnet. This is how the needles for compasses were once made.

When steel nails touch a magnet, they become temporary magnets and attract other nails. When separated from the magnet, the nails lose their magnetism.

PERMANENT MAGNETS

Permanent magnets are made of "hard" magnetic materials, such as cobalt and nickel, which tend to keep their magnetic properties forever. Materials that can become permanent magnets are called **ferromagnetic**. Examples of permanent magnets include bar magnets, refrigerator magnets, and magnets used in electric can openers.

Nature's best permanent magnet is lodestone. Permanent magnets can also be manufactured. Modern technology allows us to make powerful permanent magnets from **alloys**, or mixtures, of metals. **Ferrite magnets**, made of iron, oxygen, and other elements, are both strong and cheap to make. Ferrites are used in radio speakers, computer cables, and many other objects.

Ferrite magnets are commonly used in electronics. Here, tiny beads made of ferrite magnets looped with copper wire are arranged on a computer logic board.

ELECTROMAGNETS

In an electromagnet, magnetism is created by the flow of electricity. The most basic electromagnet is a coil of wire with an electric current flowing through it. The electric current makes the coiled wire, called a **solenoid**, a temporary magnet. The solenoid is often wrapped around an iron bar, which makes it a much stronger electromagnet. The electromagnet loses its magnetism once the electric current is turned off. Electromagnets are used in lots of devices, including telephones, doorbells, and motors.

Earth's Magnetic Field

Earth is surrounded by a vast magnetic field, which causes our planet to act like a giant bar magnet hanging in space. Chemical and electrical activity deep inside the planet produces the magnetic field.

OUR MAGNETIC PLANET

Scientists believe that Earth's magnetic field is created by the movement of molten iron deep inside the planet. The inner core, or center, of Earth is a dense, solid ball made mostly of iron and nickel. Surrounding this inner core is an outer core made of iron and nickel that is so hot, about 7,800°F (4,300°C), that it flows like liquid. The currents of molten iron, swirled around by Earth's rotation, become aligned along a north-south polar axis and create a magnetic field.

Because Earth has north and south magnetic poles, it should behave like a magnet. Opposite poles (north-south) should attract, and like poles (north-north) repel. So why does the north pole of

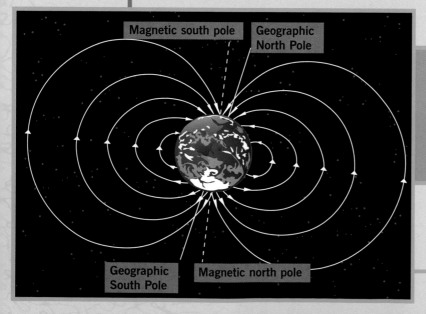

Magnetic south pole

Geographic North Pole

Geographic South Pole

Magnetic north pole

On all magnets, magnetic field lines travel from the north pole to the south pole. Earth's magnetic field lines extend from the bottom of the planet to the top.

a compass needle point north? Because the *geographic* North Pole is actually Earth's magnetic south pole. Likewise, Earth's geographic South Pole is actually its magnetic north pole. The North Pole is not named for its magnetic polarity; it is named for its location on the globe—which is north of everything else. The same applies to the South Pole.

Earth's magnetic poles move. They shift about 6 miles (10 kilometers) to 25 miles (40 kilometers) each year. Earth's magnetic south pole has wandered to as far as northeastern Canada—900 miles (1,500 kilometers) away from the geographic North Pole.

A GIANT TEARDROP

Earth's magnetic field is actually shaped like a giant teardrop around the planet. The magnetic field that extends beyond the atmosphere into space is called the **magnetosphere**. The **solar wind**, which is made of electrically charged particles flowing into space from the Sun, blows the magnetosphere into this shape. A flattened shock wave called a **bow shock** forms where the solar wind blasts into the magnetic field. The magnetic field then gradually trails off on the other side of the planet to form a tail-like **magnetotail**.

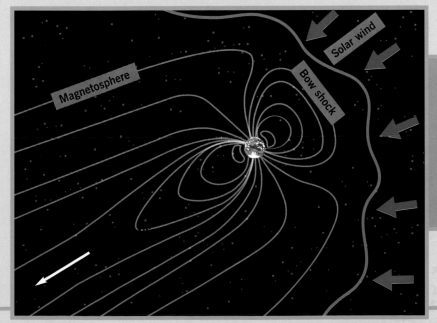

The magnetosphere is a protective shield that blocks dangerous solar winds from reaching Earth. On the opposite side of Earth, the magnetotail drags off into space thousands of miles past the orbit of the Moon.

COMPASSES

Have you ever used a compass to help you find directions? A simple pocket compass can point you north when there are no familiar landmarks to guide you. More advanced compasses are used in cars, ships, and airplanes.

The movement of a compass's needle is not only influenced by Earth's poles—it can be attracted to any magnet. At 0.5 gauss, Earth's magnetic field is very weak, far less than the magnetic field of a typical bar magnet (100 gauss). This means that even a tiny refrigerator magnet placed near your compass can easily send you in the wrong direction.

KEY EXPERIMENT Orienteering

Orienteering is the use of a compass to travel from point to point. Using a compass and tape measure, work outside in small teams to walk in the following directions for the indicated distances. As you walk, draw a picture of the path you take. You should end up where you began, so your picture should form a closed shape.

	Distance	Direction
1)	Begin	
2)	40 feet (12 meters)	N
3)	20 feet (6 meters)	NE
4)	20 feet (6 meters)	SE
5)	40 feet (12 meters)	S
6)	20 feet (6 meters)	SW
7)	20 feet (6 meters)	NW

A simple compass has a magnetized needle mounted on a pivot to allow it to freely spin around. The needle aligns itself with Earth's magnetic field and points north. A circular card under the needle is marked with 360 degrees to indicate direction. North is marked by 0 and 360 degrees, east by 90 degrees, south by 180 degrees, and west by 270 degrees.

TINY COMPASSES IN THE GROUND

Geologists, scientists who study Earth, have discovered that the planet's north and south magnetic poles repeatedly switch directions over the course of several thousands of years—north becomes south, and south becomes north. The last time this **geomagnetic reversal** occurred was 780,000 years ago.

How do geologists know this? Tiny particles of iron and other ferromagnetic substances found in rocks act like tiny compass needles. In iron-rich molten rocks, such as lava, these particles line up along the lines of force in Earth's magnetic field. When the rocks cool and harden, they leave a permanent record of the magnetic field of Earth at that time. If magnetic particles found in these rocky materials do not line up correctly with Earth's magnetic field today, then scientists know the rock formed long ago when Earth's magnetic field had a different direction.

Thousands of years from now, this lava on Hawaii might give scientists clues about the direction of Earth's magnetic poles during our lifetime.

Proof of Earth's changing magnetic field is in the striped rock on the ocean floor. Each stripe of rock contains iron that has been magnetized. Using a device called a **magnetometer**, geologists detected that the poles of one stripe of rock were opposite those in the stripe next to it. This showed that the direction of Earth's magnetic field had changed. And because the seafloor expands at a steady rate, geologists could determine when these changes occurred.

Scientists remain uncertain about when Earth's poles will reverse again. The gap in time between geomagnetic reversals is too great and too random for anyone to accurately predict.

PALEOMAGNETISM

What did Earth look like millions of years ago, and what might it look like in the future? **Paleomagnetism**, the study of the changes in Earth's magnetic field through time, helps geologists answer these questions. Geologists can use paleomagnetism to learn the age of a rock sample and determine whether the rock was once located in some other place on Earth's surface. They do this by studying the rock's magnetic history. They look at the arrangement of magnetic minerals in the rock to determine the direction and strength of its original magnetic field. Knowing how Earth's magnetic field has changed over time, scientists can estimate the age and origin of rocks and fossils everywhere on the planet.

DRIFTING CONTINENTS

Paleomagnetism has revealed that pieces of Earth's surface are in different places today than they once were. This helped verify the theory of **plate tectonics**, which explains the movement of Earth's crust. Tectonic plates are giant slabs of crust 60 miles (100 kilometers) thick that ride on top of Earth's mantle. Tectonic plates form Earth's continents and ocean floor. As the plates have moved, they have carried the continents to new locations on the globe, causing the map of Earth to change dramatically. More than 200 million years ago, all of Earth's continents were joined together in a gigantic landmass named Pangaea. Over millions of years, the continents broke up and gradually drifted to their present locations—a process called **continental drift**.

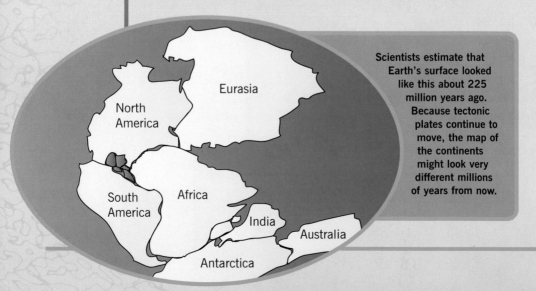

North America

Eurasia

South America

Africa

India

Australia

Antarctica

Scientists estimate that Earth's surface looked like this about 225 million years ago. Because tectonic plates continue to move, the map of the continents might look very different millions of years from now.

SCIENCE PIONEERS Alfred Wegener: Continental Drift

German **meteorologist** Alfred Wegener (1880–1930) was the first scientist to propose that the continents drift across Earth's surface. In 1912, he published a study that showed how the shapes of the continents fit together like pieces of a jigsaw puzzle. He also noted that scientists had found the fossils of similar animals in South America and Africa. He concluded from this evidence that all the continents once formed one large supercontinent until they drifted apart. Most other scientists opposed the idea of continental drift until the 1960s, when more evidence, including paleomagnetism, convinced them that Wegener was correct.

AURORAS

You can see signs of Earth's magnetic field in the sky, too. **Auroras** are beautiful displays of colored lights that glow in the night sky in far northern areas and far southern areas. Auroras appear when electrically charged particles in the solar wind interact with the strongest spots of the planet's magnetic field, near the north and south poles. When the charged particles collide with atoms in the atmosphere, energy is released as light.

Auroras that appear near the northern polar areas are called aurora borealis. Those that appear in southern polar areas are aurora australis.

HOW ANIMALS USE EARTH'S MAGNETIC FIELD

The magnetic field at the surface of Earth has a strength of only about 0.5 gauss—far too weak for humans to detect without special instruments. Many animals, however, have the natural ability to detect and use this field.

Many kinds of birds fly vast distances during their spring and fall seasonal journeys, called migrations. Scientists believe that the birds use Earth's magnetic field to guide them during these long trips. Scientists have found tiny particles of magnetite inside the brains of pigeons, robins, terns, and other birds. These particles line up with Earth's magnetic field lines and act as internal compasses that help the birds follow the correct flight paths.

Scientists have discovered magnetite in the bodies of other animals, including honeybees, salmon, tuna, sea turtles, and dolphins. All these animals travel great distances or exhibit other behaviors in which knowledge of directions is important.

Swimming furiously upstream, salmon travel hundreds of miles to lay their eggs in the same spot where they were born. Scientists believe that the magnetite in salmon's brains acts as a compass needle to help these fish find their way home.

Did you know...?

Humans have tiny amounts of magnetite in a small bone in our noses. However, we do not have the highly developed magnetic sense that animals do. We need maps and compasses to guide us.

SHARK DETECTORS

Sharks have a different biological compass than migrating creatures that rely on magnetite in their bodies to help them navigate. Sharks have sensing organs on their heads and faces that help them detect changes in electromagnetic fields.

These organs are sensitive enough to detect the weak electric fields produced by the muscle contractions of fish. Sharks use these receptors not only to track down prey but also to find their way through the ocean. By following paths outlined by magnetic fields on the ocean floor, sharks can travel thousands of miles without getting lost. When ocean currents move across a magnetic field in the ocean floor, they generate a weak electric field that the shark uses for navigation.

KEY EXPERIMENT Homing Pigeons and Earth's Magnetic Field

In 1981, German scientists conducted an experiment to study how homing pigeons find their way home. The scientists released different groups of pigeons away from their homes on sunny days, some with magnets glued to their backs. The normal pigeons headed for home without any trouble. The pigeons with the magnets, however, flew off in many different directions. The magnets interfered with the birds' ability to sense Earth's magnetic field. The scientists concluded that sensing Earth's magnetic field is a more important guide than seeing the position of the Sun for pigeons trying to find their way home.

Electromagnetism

In 1820, Danish scientist Hans Christian Oersted (1777–1851) proved that an electric current running through a metal wire could produce a magnetic field. His discovery was clear evidence that magnetism and electricity were related, and it marked a turning point in the study of electromagnetism.

Oersted later wound the metal wire into coils to create a solenoid. British physicist William Sturgeon (1783–1850) later discovered that placing an iron bar inside a solenoid greatly increased the strength of the magnetic field. A third scientist, Joseph Henry (1797–1878), found that adding insulation to the wire made the electromagnet many times stronger. Finally in 1832, Henry produced an electromagnet powerful enough to lift 3,600 pounds (1,633 kilograms)—about the weight of a small modern car.

Today's electromagnets are even stronger, and they give power to more devices than their inventors ever could have imagined.

A powerful electromagnet at a recycling center can haul tons of scrap metal at a time. Because an electromagnet runs on an electric current, its magnetic field can easily be turned on or off.

FOUR FUNDAMENTAL FORCES

Electromagnetism is one of the four fundamental forces of the universe. The other three are gravity, the **weak nuclear force**, and the **strong nuclear force**.

Gravity is the force of attraction between all objects. It attracts planets and stars to each other and keeps our feet planted on Earth. The weak nuclear force causes the radioactive decay of atomic nuclei. In this process, a chemical element breaks down into a different element. The strong nuclear force holds the nucleus of an atom together.

ELECTRIC CURRENTS AND MAGNETIC FIELDS

Of course, we cannot see the magnetic field that is created when an electric current flows through a wire. But we can determine the direction of the magnetic lines of force and the position of the magnetic poles by using the so-called right-hand rule. Imagine you are holding an insulated wire in your right hand, with your thumb pointing in the direction of the electric current. Your thumb would point toward the north pole of the magnetic field. Your other fingers would curl around the wire in the direction of the magnetic field.

Applying the right-hand rule will tell you the direction of the magnetic lines of force in a wire.

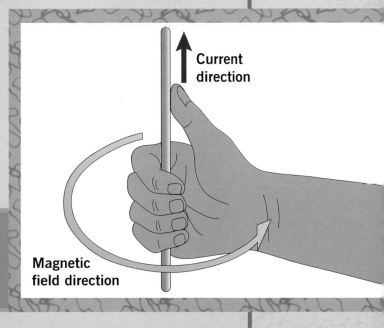

Current direction

Magnetic field direction

ELECTROMAGNETS

Most electromagnets have a core of soft iron, which makes the magnet thousands of times stronger. Other ways to increase the power of an electromagnet include increasing the amount of electric current flowing through it and increasing the number of coils in the wire. An electromagnet has a north pole and a south pole located at either end of the wire coil. The direction of the magnetic field depends on the flow of the electric current.

GALVANOMETERS

Scientists use **galvanometers** to detect and measure small electric currents. In a galvanometer, an electric current flowing through a wire in the presence of a magnetic field produces a measurable force in the wire.

A typical galvanometer has a scale with a zero in the center and numbers on either side. An indicator on the galvanometer—either a needle or a beam of light—moves to one side of zero when a current passes through the device. A current in the opposite direction causes the indicator to move to the other side of the zero. The stronger the current, the farther the indicator moves on the scale.

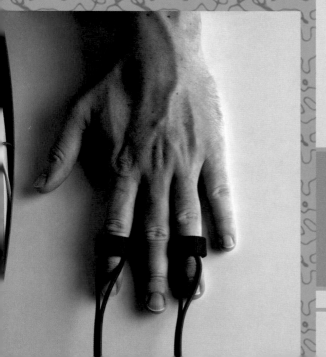

Galvanometers can detect electrical activity produced by the human heart. Galvanometers have also been used in such devices as **polygraph machines**, also known as lie detectors. A polygraph can detect whether a criminal suspect is lying or telling the truth.

This polygraph machine uses galvanometers connected to fingerplates to measure the amount of electricity conducted by the fingers. If a person becomes nervous and sweats, the skin will conduct more electricity than it does when dry. Changes in the amount of electricity conducted are detected by the galvanometers and recorded on the computer screen.

ELECTRIC MOTORS

To better understand the relationship between magnets and electricity, it helps to know how an electric motor works. A motor turns electrical energy into mechanical energy (motion).

A motor typically has an iron cylinder, called an **armature**, attached to a shaft between the north and south poles of a permanent magnet. The armature is wrapped in a metal coil. When an electric current is sent through the coil, the armature becomes an electromagnet with north and south poles.

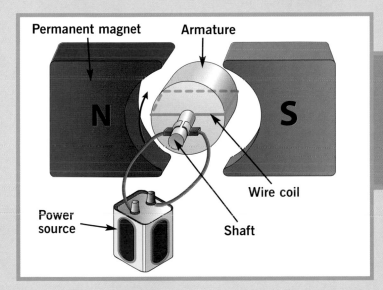

Permanent magnet   Armature

N   S

Wire coil

Power source

Shaft

The continuous reversal of the magnetic poles in the armature causes a cycle of half rotations that gives the motor its power.

The north pole of the magnetized armature is repelled by the north pole of the permanent magnet. In turn, the armature spins toward the magnet's south pole, completing half a rotation. Just as the north pole of the armature reaches the south pole of the permanent magnet, the electric current to the armature is reversed. This reverses the poles of the armature— its north pole becomes south.

The armature's south pole is repelled by the permanent magnet's south pole, causing it to spin toward the north pole. The current continues to switch, reversing the poles, at the precise moment the armature makes each half turn. This keeps the armature constantly spinning and makes the motor run.

MAGNETS IN EVERYDAY LIFE

So what role does electromagnetism play in our day-to-day lives? For the answer, simply look around at the appliances and machines in your home. Washing machines, blenders, vacuum cleaners, hair dryers, CD and DVD players, computers, fax machines, printers, power tools, toy robots—basically anything with moving parts and an electric motor—all have magnets to make them operate.

COMPUTERS

A computer is just one example of an everyday device that uses magnets. If you were to look inside a computer, you would find a hard disk that stores all your computer's software and data. This disk spins beneath a small metal part called a read/write head, which is extended from a metallic arm. The head is an electromagnet that can read and record information as tiny magnetic particles on the disk. The platter is made of glass or aluminum with tiny magnetic particles.

When the head is recording data, or "writing," its magnetic field arranges the magnetic particles into patterns that represent pictures or sound. When "reading," the head converts these patterns into electrical signals. Other magnets in the computer convert these signals back into pictures or sound.

In a typical computer, the read/write head scans the hard disk platter more than 50 times per second!

RECENT DEVELOPMENTS Magnetic Refrigerators

Refrigerators no longer just hang magnets—now they can be *made* of magnets. A magnetic refrigerator has a cooling system that chills the inside of the refrigerator with a magnet. A regular refrigerator lowers the temperature using a gas that liquifies easily when compressed; the liquid then removes heat from the refrigerator when it turns back into a gas. But the magnetic version uses a permanent magnet and a special metal called gadolinium. When this metal is exposed to a magnetic field, it cools. The cooling of the metal, in turn, causes water flowing around it to cool. The cool water moves through tubes to chill the inside of the refrigerator.

MICROPHONES

A microphone also works with electromagnets. Sound waves cause vibrations in the air, and a microphone converts these vibrations into corresponding electrical signals. Inside the microphone is a diaphragm— a thin, flexible sheet of metal or plastic—that is attached to a coil of wire. The coil is either attached to or wrapped around a magnet. Sound waves cause the diaphragm to vibrate, which in turn causes the wire coil to vibrate. The wire's changing position in relation to the magnet causes a current to flow through the wire. This audio current can be amplified, transmitted, or **encoded** and then stored on a magnetic tape or disk. To hear the recorded sounds, the encoded data is converted into electrical signals, sent through a loudspeaker, and converted back into vibrations of sound.

When sound waves enter a microphone, an electromagnet helps convert the sound into electrical signals that we hear through speakers.

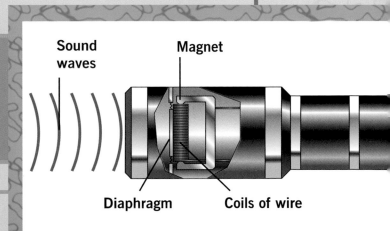

Sound waves

Magnet

Diaphragm

Coils of wire

MAGNETS CREATE ELECTRICITY

After Oersted proved that an electric current could turn a metal wire into a magnet, scientists began to wonder whether the reverse could be true. Could a magnet create electricity?

More than a decade after Oersted's discovery, British chemist Michael Faraday (1791–1867) came up with an answer. Faraday was doing an experiment with an electromagnet and a galvanometer, which measures electrical activity. He noticed that every time he switched his electromagnet on or off, the needle in the galvanometer would move. The needle did not move when the electromagnet was on—only when it was switched on or off. This led Faraday to conclude that a changing magnetic field would induce, or cause, an electric current. This process is called **electromagnetic induction**.

ELECTROMAGNETIC INDUCTION

Faraday did more experiments with magnets and electricity. In one, he discovered that when he moved a magnet near—or pulled a magnet away from—a closed loop of wire, an electric current was created in the wire. He also found that he could control the direction of the current depending on whether he moved the magnet toward the loop of wire or pulled it away.

These discoveries would later be applied in all sorts of devices. Today, electromagnetic induction is used in everything from rechargeable batteries to the enormous power generators that send electricity into our homes.

Did you know...?

Although Michael Faraday is credited with discovering electromagnetic induction in 1831, American physicist Joseph Henry made the same discovery at about the same time. Faraday was the first to publish his findings, leading to greater acclaim at the time. Henry's work, however, led to the invention of the first practical electric motor.

ELECTRIC GENERATORS

If you were to follow the electric power lines from your home to the source, you would likely find an electric generator at the other end. Electric generators power millions of homes through electromagnetic induction. Unlike an electric motor, which turns electrical energy into mechanical energy (motion), a generator turns mechanical energy into electrical energy.

A very basic generator has a wire loop mounted on a metal rod. As the wire is rotated by a handle on the rod, it enters and exits the magnetic field of a permanent magnet that surrounds it. The changes in the magnetic field induce an electric current in the wire.

The same principle is used on a larger scale in power stations. There, steam or running water (mechanical energy) rotates a **turbine**, which spins large electromagnets encased in wire coils. The electric current induced by the changing magnetic field in the wire is carried out of the generator to homes.

Because the current changes direction each time the wire coils enter or exit the magnetic field, an **alternating current** (AC) is generated. The generator's speed and current are controlled so that the current changes direction 120 times each second.

In this generator, turning the handle (mechanical energy) induces the current that powers the lightbulb (electrical energy).

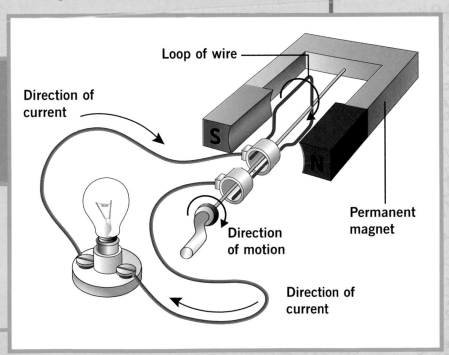

Loop of wire

Direction of current

S

N

Direction of motion

Permanent magnet

Direction of current

TRANSFORMERS

A **transformer** is a simple device used to adjust the **voltage** of an alternating current. You can think of voltage as the force that pushes a current through a wire. A transformer functions much like the nozzle of a garden hose—increasing or decreasing the force of the current. Transformers play an important role in transmitting electricity from high-voltage power lines to the 120-volt outlets in most homes. They also work with various kinds of electrical devices, from doorbells to guitar amplifiers.

A basic transformer consists of two insulated wire coils—a primary coil and a secondary coil—wrapped around an iron core. Alternating current flows into the primary coil, creating a magnetic field. Because the current is alternating, the magnetic field fluctuates, inducing a current in the secondary coil through the process of electromagnetic induction.

If the secondary coil has more loops than the primary coil, the transformer will increase, or "step up," the voltage of the current that is transmitted. If the secondary coil has fewer loops than the primary coil, the transformer will decrease, or "step down," the voltage of the current.

The metal cylinders you see near the top of utility poles are step-down transformers. The transformers decrease the high-voltage current coming from the overhead wires. Separate wires carry the lower-voltage current into our homes.

Did you know...?

Thomas Edison (1847–1931) patented the first electrical power station in the United States. New York's Pearl Street Station opened for business in 1882 and sent electricity to 59 homes. The Edison Electric Illuminating Company eventually merged with the Consolidated Gas Company to form the Consolidated Edison Company. This company, commonly known as Con Ed, now serves more than three million customers in New York City and nearby Westchester County, New York.

SUPER MAGNETS

There are two types of electromagnets: **resistive magnets** and **superconducting magnets**. Resistive magnets are ordinary electromagnets that lose energy as heat as electric current passes through their wire coils. Superconducting magnets, on the other hand, experience almost no **resistance**—electricity flows freely through them. These magnets use coils made of superconducting materials kept at very cool temperatures, so they do not lose energy as heat. As a result, superconducting magnets can produce very strong magnetic fields with the input of very little electricity.

Because their magnetic fields are so strong, superconducting magnet systems are very useful. For example, they are used in many types of scientific and medical research, including magnetic resonance imaging (MRI). In MRI, magnetic fields and radio waves produce images of tissues inside the body.

HYBRID MAGNETS

The most powerful electromagnets, called **hybrid magnets**, can generate magnetic fields with strengths of more than 450,000 gauss (45 tesla). Hybrid magnets are made by combining a resistive magnet with a superconducting magnet. In one hybrid design, the superconducting magnet encircles the resistive magnet in a structure 22 feet (6.7 meters) tall. Much of the structure is devoted to cooling the hybrid's superconducting magnet, which must be kept as low as -452°F (-269°C).

MAGNETIC LEVITATION

We know that like poles (north-north or south-south) repel each other. The force created by repelling magnets (repulsion) can be used to make objects **levitate**, or float, in the air. To produce levitation, the upward magnetic force must be stronger than the downward force of gravity.

DIAMAGNETIC LEVITATION

One form of levitation that involves magnetism is **diamagnetic** levitation. Materials such as wood, water, plants, and animals—normally thought to be nonmagnetic—are actually diamagnetic. Diamagnetic materials repel magnets, and if the repulsive force is strong enough, they can cause levitation.

All materials have a diamagnetic force—a force that repels magnetic fields—but in most materials this force is so weak that it goes unnoticed. Diamagnetic levitation is visible proof that the force exists.

When in the presence of a strong magnetic field, the atoms of diamagnetic materials undergo a certain change. The electrons in the atoms rearrange themselves in such a way that they repel the magnetic field of the nearby magnet. If the magnet is strong enough, the repulsive force can lift, or levitate, the diamagnetic material. Even humans could be levitated if placed in a strong enough magnetic field.

KEY EXPERIMENT Floating Frog

In a famous 1997 experiment, a powerful 16-tesla electromagnet was used to make a live frog float in the air! Physicist Andrey Geim conducted the experiment at the Nijmegen High Field Magnet Laboratory in the Netherlands to demonstrate diamagnetism. The frog was placed in the hollow of a cone-shaped electromagnet. The frog's weak diamagnetic force repelled the powerful electromagnet's force just enough to counterbalance the force of gravity. This caused the frog to levitate. The frog was unharmed.

When certain metals, such as tin and aluminum, are cooled below a critical temperature, typically -423°F (-253°C), they become superconductors. This magnet is able to float because the diamagnetic force of the superconductor repels the force of the magnet just enough to counterbalance the force of gravity.

SUPERCONDUCTING LEVITATION

A **superconductor** is the most diamagnetic of all materials. It expels, or kicks out, its interior magnetic field, and it repels any other magnetic field. Some superconductors, however, have tiny defects that permit just enough magnetism to enable superconducting levitation to occur.

In superconducting levitation, a magnet is lifted into the air and suspended in place. The levitation occurs because the superconductor is diamagnetic—it repels the magnet—and the force is stronger than gravity. The magnet remains suspended because its magnetic field is essentially trapped in place by the superconductor.

The principles of superconducting levitation are used in the design of certain types of magnetic levitation trains—trains that are suspended or guided by magnetic force.

MAGLEV TRAINS

Magnetic levitation, or maglev, trains rely on powerful electromagnets to levitate above a track or guideway. Maglev trains are propelled by a linear motor—an electric motor in which the magnetic fields produced by the motor move objects along a straight path.

Like all moving objects, trains that have wheels and run along a track are slowed by **friction**. Think of friction as the force that opposes the push or pull of another force—in this case, a train that speeds along a track. Without the friction that occurs when the wheels of ordinary trains rub against the track, maglev trains can travel faster than 300 miles (483 kilometers) per hour.

HOW MAGLEVS WORK

Here's how one maglev system works: The bottom part of the train's frame is curved and wraps around a T-shaped guideway. Magnets in the frame are attracted upward toward magnets in the guideway. The force of attraction is monitored so that the train is lifted just enough to keep it suspended 10 millimeters above the guideway.

This maglev train in Shanghai, China, was the first commercial maglev train in operation. The train shuttles passengers to and from Pudong International Airport at a maximum speed of 268 miles (431 kilometers) per hour.

Did you know...?

In December 2003, an experimental maglev train in Japan set a new maglev speed record of 361 miles (581 kilometers) per hour.

To propel the train, alternating current surges through electromagnetic coils in the guideway walls, interacting with magnets on the train. Alternating current creates a moving magnetic field, pushing and pulling the train forward using a sequence of alternating magnetic poles.

Alternating magnetic poles are what make the armature of an electric motor spin. In this case, however, the magnets are linear (in a line), not circular, so the train moves forward like a surfer riding an ocean wave.

RECENT DEVELOPMENTS Pittsburgh's Maglev Train

The next stop for the maglev train may be Pittsburgh. The Pennsylvania High-Speed Maglev Project is planning a 54-mile (87-kilometer) maglev line connecting Pittsburgh's airport to the city's downtown and surrounding suburbs. For Pittsburgh, the train would ease traffic congestion, reduce pollution, bring new business to the area, and reduce travel time from downtown to the suburbs.

Pittsburgh is located about halfway between New York and Chicago. One day, the train line may be extended to 500 miles (800 kilometers), linking Pittsburgh to those cities and many others as well. If so, it would serve about half of the U.S. population and more than half of the country's largest markets. However, maglev train systems are expensive to build, and the train lines cross public and private land that is used for other purposes. Before the trains are built, people in the affected communities must agree that the benefits of the trains outweigh the costs.

Electromagnetic Radiation

Disturbances in electromagnetic fields create waves of energy. These waves are known as **electromagnetic radiation** because the waves radiate, or spread out, from the motion of the electrically charged particles. Some electromagnetic waves form visible light—the light from the Sun and from lamps. Other kinds of electromagnetic waves are invisible, such as those in X-ray machines and microwave ovens. These waves can pass through air, empty space, and other substances.

ELECTROMAGNETIC WAVES

Electromagnetic waves are like the waves on the surface of a pond that are created by tossing a stone into the water. Electromagnetic waves travel outward from the source of radiation at the speed of light—186,282 miles (299,792 kilometers) per second.

Like the waves in a pond, electromagnetic waves have such features as **wavelength**, **frequency**, and **amplitude**. Wavelength is the distance from the peak (high spot) of one wave to the peak of the next. Frequency is the number of times per second that the peaks pass a certain point. Amplitude is the distance from a peak or trough (low point) to the midpoint of the wave.

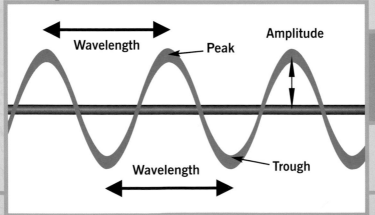

All types of waves have the same characteristics that can be measured: wavelength, frequency, and amplitude.

ELECTROMAGNETIC SPECTRUM

The different types of electromagnetic waves are spread out in a band of energy called the **electromagnetic spectrum**. The type of wave is determined by its wavelength and frequency. The shorter the wavelength, and the greater the frequency, the greater the energy of the wave.

Light from the Sun or a lightbulb is made of medium-sized wavelengths—located in the middle of the spectrum. This is called visible light because it is the only electromagnetic radiation that can be seen by the human eye. Its position in the spectrum is called the **visible spectrum**.

Other types of electromagnetic radiation (ranging from shortest wavelength to longest) are gamma rays, X-rays, ultraviolet rays (UV), infrared rays, microwaves, and radio waves.

All electromagnetic waves travel at the same speed—the speed of light. Differing wavelengths and frequencies are what separates one type from another.

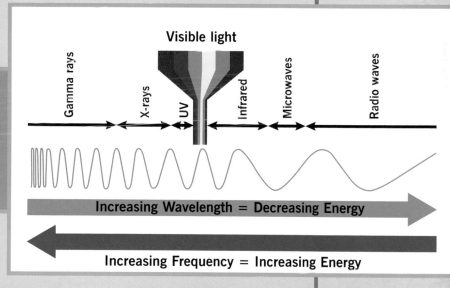

PHOTONS

In addition to behaving like waves, electromagnetic radiation also moves as pointlike particles called photons. These particles of energy move like billiard balls rolling across the surface of a pool table. All forms of electromagnetic radiation behave like both waves and particles, depending on the experiment used to observe them.

GAMMA RAYS

Gamma rays have the shortest wavelength, highest frequency, and greatest amount of energy of all forms of electromagnetic radiation. Gamma rays are given off by radioactive atoms as these atoms break down to form different elements. Sources of gamma rays include the element uranium, which is used to produce energy in nuclear power plants. Other gamma rays come from the Sun, from exploding stars called **supernovae**, and from **nebulae**, which are cosmic clouds of gas and dust.

Tiny amounts of gamma rays are constantly entering our bodies from naturally radioactive material all around us, including chemical compounds in the air and soil. These rays are normally harmless. In large amounts, however, gamma rays can cause changes in the body's cells that lead to cancer and other diseases. But they can also be beneficial. Gamma rays that are focused on cancer cells can destroy them, helping to treat cancer in patients.

Astronomers have found that the highest-energy gamma rays ever detected come from the Crab Nebula. The Crab Nebula is a giant cloud of gas and dust that was created by a supernova. Chinese astronomers wrote about seeing this supernova in the year 1054.

X-RAYS

If you've ever been to a doctor or dentist, you might have seen X-ray pictures of parts of your body. X-rays can pass through your body to make photographic images of your bones, teeth, and other tissues. Such images allow doctors and dentists to diagnose and treat medical problems.

X-rays are produced by an X-ray tube. The tube directs the X-rays at a specific body part. X-rays can pass through your body tissues but not through your bones or teeth. The rays that pass through your body are detected on sheets of special film or plastic to make photographs of your bones, teeth, or internal organs. Your bones and teeth absorb the rays, so those areas show up as white on the resulting image.

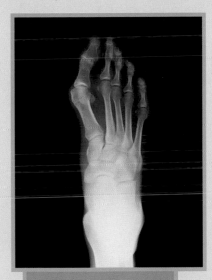

This X-ray shows a lump called a bunion on a patient's big toe.

X-rays can cause damage to living cells. To prevent this kind of damage, doctors and dentists often cover the parts of the patient's body that are not being examined with a shield made from lead. Lead absorbs more X-rays than most other substances, so it acts as a barrier that protects the parts of the body that are not being examined.

OTHER USES FOR X-RAYS

You may have also noticed X-ray machines at airports. Security workers at airports scan luggage with X-rays to look for bombs, illegal drugs, and other items inside the luggage. Manufacturers use X-rays to check for flaws inside products, including steel items and computer chips.

ULTRAVIOLET RAYS

Ultraviolet (UV) rays are a form of invisible light that comes from the Sun, lightning, and various objects in space. Too much exposure to UV radiation can cause painful sunburn and even skin cancer. Too much UV radiation can also damage your eyes.

Most of the Sun's harmful UV rays are blocked from reaching Earth's surface by a layer of oxygen in the upper atmosphere called the ozone layer. Some of the ozone layer is thinner than it should be because of **chlorofluorocarbons (CFCs)**. CFCs are compounds that used to be used in many common household products, such as refrigerators and aerosol cans. When CFCs drift into the upper atmosphere, they react with ozone and break it down. The extra UV rays penetrating through this "ozone hole" pose a health threat to people and other animals.

CASE STUDY Sunburn

Severe sunburn can cause aging of the skin and even skin cancer. Protect yourself from harmful UV rays by applying sunscreen to your skin. Sunscreens contain two types of ingredients that protect your skin. One type reflects UV rays away from your body, and the other absorbs UV rays. The effectiveness of different sunscreens is measured in numbers called sun protection factors (SPFs). Sunscreens with SPFs of 15 or higher are most effective.

BENEFICIAL UV RAYS

Moderate exposure to ultraviolet rays is good for you. It helps your body produce vitamin D, which is needed for bone strength. Physicians expose some patients to limited amounts of UV rays to help manage such skin conditions as acne and psoriasis.

Even the harmful effects of UV rays can be useful. Lamps that emit UV radiation can be used in hospitals to kill bacteria and other microbes on surgical instruments. Food and drug companies also use UV rays to kill germs in their products.

VISIBLE LIGHT

Visible light makes up just a tiny part of the electromagnetic spectrum. Nevertheless, it is vital to our lives. Visible light emits waves of medium length, which are detected by the human eye and converted into colors by the brain.

LIGHT FROM NUCLEAR FUSION

Light photons are made in **nuclear fusion** reactions in the Sun's core. In nuclear fusion, matter is converted into energy when the nuclei of atoms combine. This process gives off photons, which travel to the Sun's surface, where they excite atoms. When these atoms return to their original energy levels, they emit the extra energy as light photons. This is the light that we see coming from the Sun.

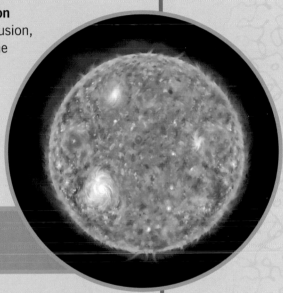

At the Sun's core, massive pressure and extreme temperatures force atomic nuclei to fuse, or join together, and release energy.

RECENT DEVELOPMENTS ITER

Construction has begun on a nuclear fusion reactor called ITER, which will produce energy using the same force that powers the Sun. In nuclear fusion, hydrogen atoms are heated to super-high temperatures, which fuses the nuclei of the atoms and creates plasma—a hot, electrically charged gas. Plasma generates energy but is very unstable; controlling it is like trying to maintain the shape of a water balloon. To stabilize the plasma, ITER will surround it with a magnetic field inside a superconducting electromagnet. If scientists succeed, they will be much closer to making nuclear fusion a safe, renewable energy source.

INFRARED RAYS

Although infrared waves are invisible, you can feel them in the form of heat. The Sun radiates infrared waves, along with visible light and ultraviolet waves.

All objects, even your own body, give off infrared radiation. Warmer objects emit more infrared radiation than cooler objects do. When an object such as the filament in a lightbulb or the surface of the Sun becomes very warm, it gives off both infrared rays and visible light. The heat-generating properties of infrared waves have many uses, including melting ice from airplane wings and keeping food warm.

CASE STUDY Remote Controls

Remote controls use infrared radiation. An electronic circuit inside your television remote control senses when you press a button to change the channel. Then, a small lightbulb called a light-emitting diode (LED) shoots rays of infrared light with coded signals. The infrared light is picked up and decoded by a receiver in your TV, which causes the channel to change.

Special cameras, binoculars, and telescopes enable people to see infrared radiation. If you had your picture taken with an infrared camera, you would see your body glowing with light. Night-vision goggles make infrared rays visible and help police, firefighters, and military personnel find people in dark or smoky places. Such devices are also used by wildlife scientists and hunters to find animals at night.

A thermogram is an infrared image taken with a special camera. This thermogram shows a girl playing a video game. The warmest areas, such as the girl's skin, are shown in white, and the coolest areas are shown in blue and purple.

MICROWAVES

Microwaves are familiar to most people for quick cooking in microwave ovens. When water molecules in food absorb microwaves, the molecules start to vibrate quickly. The vibration causes molecules to hit and spin each other, and this energy produces heat. This is the heat that cooks the food in microwave ovens.

Microwaves are actually a type of radio wave. Their wavelengths are much longer than those of other types of electromagnetic radiation, but they are shorter than those of other radio waves. Like all radio waves, microwaves can easily pass through rain, smoke, gas, dust, and other material without interference. These properties make microwaves useful in radar systems and for long-distance communication, such as in some cell phones and wireless computer networks. Scientists use microwaves to communicate with distant satellites and other spacecraft.

Cell phones and wireless Internet networks use microwave frequencies to connect with each other.

CLUES TO THE EARLY UNIVERSE

Two satellite telescopes—the Cosmic Background Explorer (COBE) and the Wilkinson Microwave Anisotropy Probe (WMAP)—have provided astronomers with much information about the early universe by measuring cosmic microwave background (CMB) radiation. The CMB radiation is microwave energy left over from the Big Bang, the explosion that gave birth to the universe about 13.7 billion years ago. Scientists now use their knowledge of CMB radiation to conduct a wide range of experiments and to study the structure of the universe.

RADIO WAVES

You can listen to your favorite radio station because your radio's antenna receives electromagnetic waves broadcast by the radio station. The radio has magnets and other electronic parts that convert this electromagnetic radiation back into sounds.

WAVELENGTHS AND FREQUENCIES

There are different kinds of radio waves, each with different wavelengths and frequencies (or speeds). High-frequency radio waves move faster than low-frequency waves and can transmit more information. High-frequency radio waves also require shorter antennas. For these reasons, most forms of telecommunication use radio waves with medium to high frequencies.

Cordless phones, some cell phones, and many television systems, including high-definition TV, transmit radio waves in ultrahigh frequencies (UHF). FM (frequency modulation) radio stations and other television systems use very high frequency (VHF) radio waves. AM (amplitude modulation) radio stations use medium frequencies. However, low-frequency radio waves are important too. Submarines, for instance, use very slow, very long radio waves to communicate with people on land, because these radio waves can pass through shallow water.

AM AND FM RADIO

The speed of FM radio waves ranges from 88 to 108 megahertz (million **hertz**). This is why the FM dial on your radio goes from 88 to 108. Likewise, the AM dial on your radio goes from 550 to 1600 because AM radio waves range from 550 to 1,600 kilohertz (thousand hertz).

Did you know...?

In 1895, Guglielmo Marconi (1874–1937) broadcast the first radio communication signals through the air. Marconi's signals were a series of clicks, like those used in telegraph communication.

NAVIGATION

Navigators on airplanes and ships use radio waves to help them stay on course. In the past, pilots used signals from AM radio stations to navigate the night skies. Today, pilots use Global Positioning Systems (GPS) for navigation. A satellite in orbit around Earth sends radio waves to an aircraft's GPS receiver, which calculates the aircraft's position. Many of today's automobiles are also equipped with GPS technology.

Did you know...?

Voyager 1 is the most distant human-made object in the universe. It is still sending radio waves to Earth after crossing the "termination shock" in 2005. The termination shock is the edge of the solar system, where the pressure of particles streaming from the Sun equals the pressure of particles from other stars. The distance from Earth to *Voyager 1* is about 95 times the distance from Earth to the Sun.

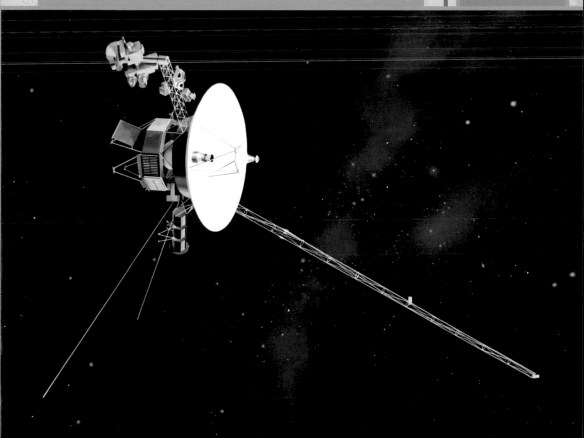

Scientists use radio waves to communicate with distant spacecraft, such as *Voyager 1*, which is on the very edge of our solar system.

Special Uses of Magnets and Electromagnetic Radiation

Magnetism and electromagnetic radiation are used in so many common, everyday devices that people rarely think about them. Medical personnel, manufacturers, and scientists also use magnets and electromagnetic radiation in many different ways.

MEDICINE

Hospitals have many kinds of machines that help doctors see inside the human body. These machines produce images that make it easier for doctors to diagnose and treat patients. Radiology is the field of medicine in which electromagnetic radiation is used to make images. Doctors who make and interpret such images are called radiologists. Radiologists help doctors treat broken bones, torn ligaments, blood clots, and even cancer.

CASE STUDY Radiation Therapy and Cancer

Radiation therapy is used to treat cancer patients. In this therapy, high doses of gamma rays and X-rays are directed at the cancer cells. The powerful electromagnetic waves destroy the genetic material in the cancer cells, making it impossible for the cells to grow and divide. Normal cells may also be damaged in this therapy, but doctors try to harm as few of the normal cells as possible. Radiation therapy may be used before surgery, during surgery, after surgery, and in combination with drug treatment.

CASE STUDY Magnet Therapy?

Some people claim that exposure to small magnets has a variety of health benefits, such as improved blood circulation, relief from pain and swelling, and faster recovery from injuries. However, careful scientific studies show little evidence for such benefits from magnets. The United States Food and Drug Administration (FDA) warns companies against making health claims for magnets that are not supported by scientific evidence.

MAGNETIC RESONANCE IMAGING

Doctors use X-ray machines to examine bones. But to examine soft tissue around the bones, such as cartilage, ligaments, and even brain tissue, they rely on magnetic resonance imaging (MRI). MRI machines use a large magnet, radio waves, and a computer to make pictures of tissue inside the body. First, a magnetic field causes atomic nuclei inside the tissue to line up in a certain way. Radio waves are then focused on these nuclei, and the nuclei absorb the energy of the waves. When the radio waves stop, the nuclei go back to their original positions. They give off the extra energy as radio signals. The MRI machine detects these signals, and a computer changes them into pictures of the tissue.

MRI technology can detect brain tumors, torn cartilage and ligaments, nerve damage associated with diseases such as multiple sclerosis, and abnormalities in arteries that can lead to heart attacks and dangerous blood clots.

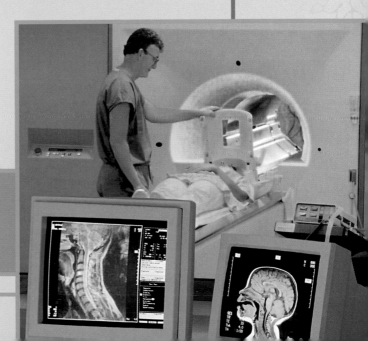

When being examined by an MRI machine, the patient is often placed inside a small chamber of a large electromagnet. The effect of the magnetic field on the body is read and translated into an image, which appears on the computer screen.

POSITRON EMISSION TOMOGRAPHY

Different kinds of radiation are required for different medical needs. Positron emission tomography (PET) is used to make images of the chemical activity inside the brain and other body tissues. For a PET scan, a person is injected with a small amount of a radioactive substance, which the blood carries to the brain. This substance causes brain cells to emit gamma rays. These rays are detected by special cameras and converted into images by a computer. Doctors often use PET to learn about chemical changes in the brains of patients with Alzheimer's disease, epilepsy, and other disorders.

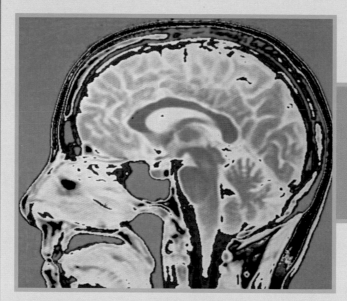

A look inside the brain provided by a PET scan helps doctors detect chemical changes that might be linked to a disease.

COMPUTED TOMOGRAPHY

Computed tomography (CT), also known as computerized axial tomography (CAT), uses X-rays to make detailed images of the body's interior. Beams of X-rays are aimed at the patient from different angles, creating many different images of a body part. A computer combines all the images into a single three-dimensional (3-D) image. Doctors can rotate such images on computer screens to examine the body part from different angles. This helps them diagnose such conditions as tumors, blood clots, and broken bones.

IRRADIATION

Electromagnetic radiation can change the structure of cells and even destroy them. In a process called **irradiation**, people use gamma rays, X-rays, or UV rays to change the biological and chemical structure of objects in ways that are beneficial. For example, the medical-supply industry uses irradiation to sterilize, or remove all bacteria from, surgical instruments.

Irradiation is used in the food industry to kill germs and insects on food—a process called food irradiation, or cold pasteurization. There are different ways to irradiate food. One way is to direct electron beams directly at fruit and vegetables for a few seconds. Another way is to fire gamma rays or X-rays at the containers that hold the food. The rays penetrate far enough to kill any bacteria. In both cases, the electromagnetic rays cause atoms to become electrically charged, or **ionized**. The ionization destroys the living tissue of germs or insects, but the radiation dose is kept low enough so that the food is not harmed.

Some people oppose food irradiation because it can change the chemical and nutritional makeup of food, and exposes food to radiation. However, testing indicates that irradiated food does not pose a risk to public health. According to the U.S. Centers for Disease Control and Prevention, the chemical changes caused by irradiation are fewer than those caused by canning food. Also, the radiation used in the process is no stronger than that of microwave ovens.

This photo shows the difference between irradiated strawberries (left) and untreated strawberries, which have become moldy after several days.

ELECTRON MICROSCOPES

Microscopes help scientists see objects close-up, and electron microscopes let them look even closer. Electron microscopes have electromagnets that focus beams of electrons on or through a specimen to create an image of it. In one type, the electron beams cause the specimen to throw off other electrons. These "secondary" electrons are counted by a collector device, and a computer converts this count into a picture of the specimen.

An electron microscope can make a clearer picture of smaller features than a regular light microscope can. This is because the waves of the electron beam are much closer together than the waves of visible light, so the electron beam is more sensitive to tiny features. An electron microscope can magnify a specimen so much that even some individual atoms can be seen!

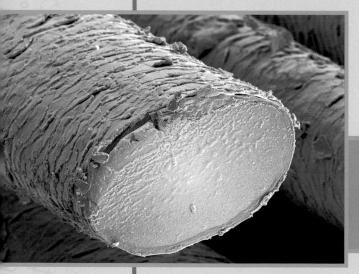

A human hair, as seen through an electron microscope, looks gigantic at 1,250 times its actual size. The electron microscope reveals tiny details that cannot be detected with an ordinary microscope.

PARTICLE ACCELERATORS

Particle accelerators, also called atom smashers, play a major role in the study of physics. These machines, some more than a mile long, can create tiny bits of matter that would be impossible to observe any other way.

Particle accelerators have powerful magnets that direct beams of atoms and subatomic particles (particles smaller than atoms) at very high speeds through a cylinder. The beams travel around the cylinder until the particles collide with each other or another target. The collision produces many new, short-lived particles that can be studied by physicists.

In some particle accelerators, a beam of electrons sends out X-rays when it passes through a magnetic field. These X-rays can be used to help make certain kinds of computer chips. Doctors sometimes use X-rays produced by particle accelerators to treat patients with cancer.

RECENT DEVELOPMENTS Large Hadron Collider

The world's longest particle accelerator facility is the CERN tunnel, near Geneva, Switzerland. This tunnel is 17 miles (27 kilometers) long. The facility's new accelerator, named the Large Hadron Collider (LHC), generates more energy than any accelerator in the world. Its length and design give it the power to collide particles such as high-energy protons and lead nuclei at the speed of light. In doing so, the LHC can recreate conditions close to the time of the Big Bang, the enormous explosion that gave birth to the universe about 13.7 billion years ago.

This is just one small section of the Large Hadron Collider (LHC). Connected to the LHC is a particle detector with the world's largest superconducting magnet, which helps scientists evaluate the effects of the particle collisions.

TELESCOPES AND SPACE PROBES

The telescopes and space probes used by scientists to explore the cosmos include electromagnets among their many components. Scientists use these telescopes and space probes to measure all forms of electromagnetic radiation in the universe. Planets, stars, nebulae, and other cosmic objects all give off different kinds of electromagnetic radiation.

Telescopes and space probes have also been used to measure gamma rays emitted by distant galaxies; X-rays given off by neutron stars (the smallest and densest kind of star); UV rays given off by quasars (very distant but very bright objects); and infrared rays emitted by star-forming nebulae. The rays emitted by these distant objects help scientists find them and track their movement.

RECENT DEVELOPMENTS Water on Mars

In 2002, the *Mars Odyssey* spacecraft orbiting Mars found evidence that there is enough ice in the first 3 feet (1 meter) of Martian soil to fill Lake Michigan twice if melted. An instrument on *Mars Odyssey* measured the energy of gamma rays blasted out of the soil by cosmic rays from space. The energy levels of the gamma rays indicated the chemical makeup of the soil. The measurements showed that there is a lot of hydrogen in the Martian ground. Scientists believe the hydrogen is most likely present as water ice, which consists of both hydrogen and oxygen.

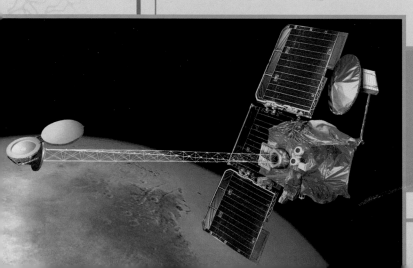

The images and data collected by *Mars Odyssey* will be used to determine possible landing sites for robots that will explore the surface of the Red Planet.

RECENT DEVELOPMENTS Search for Extraterrestrial Intelligence

The Search for Extraterrestrial Intelligence (SETI) is an international effort to find intelligent life on other planets. Researchers use radio telescopes (telescopes that detect radio waves rather than light waves) to scan nearby stars for radio signals that might be sent by intelligent beings. The radio signals are converted into digital data and analyzed by computers. Because so much computing power is needed, volunteers are asked to lend their personal computing power to the project—and SETI computers link up with the individual computers through the Internet. Computer owners interested in volunteering can sign up at the SETI website.

The Arecibo Radio Telescope in Puerto Rico, the largest radio telescope in the world, collects data for the SETI project. The telescope's massive dish is 1,000 feet (305 meters) in diameter and 167 feet (51 meters) deep. Its huge size enables the dish to collect even the faintest radio signals from space. These signals are focused on the receiver suspended 450 feet (137 meters) above the dish.

Magnetism in the Cosmos

Earth is not the only planet with a magnetic field. Scientists have learned that other planets have magnetic fields, too, as do the Sun and other celestial bodies.

MAGNETIC FIELDS OF PLANETS

No two planets are the same size or temperature. Not surprisingly, the magnetic fields of planets are different, too. Some planets have powerful magnetic fields that can be detected from Earth. Others have faint magnetic fields, detected only recently by space probes. One planet, Venus, has no magnetic field at all.

Over the last 50 years, scientists have been able to learn a great deal about the magnetism of planets, including the strength and direction of the magnetic fields and their sources of magnetism. Understanding planetary magnetism helps scientists unlock the mysteries of the planets themselves.

MERCURY

In the 1970s, the *Mariner 10* spacecraft discovered that Mercury—the smallest planet and the one closest to the Sun—has a weak magnetic field. Its magnetic field is only one percent as strong as Earth's. Mercury's magnetism comes from its large iron core. Scientists hope to learn more about Mercury in the coming years. In 2004, NASA launched the *Messenger* space probe to investigate the planet. Among the probe's missions are to map Mercury's magnetic field and to look for magnetized rock in its crust.

Mariner 10 was the first space probe to investigate Mercury. Not only did the probe detect Mercury's weak magnetic field, it also discovered that the planet's atmosphere is made up mostly of helium.

JUPITER

Jupiter, the largest planet in our solar system, also has the strongest magnetic field of all the planets. Its surface level magnetism is 14 times as strong as Earth's. Telescopes have shown glowing auroras near the poles of Jupiter. These auroras are caused by the interaction of the planet's magnetic field with charged particles from the Sun and from volcanoes on Jupiter's moons.

In the 1990s, the *Galileo* spacecraft discovered that one of Jupiter's moons, Ganymede, also produces its own magnetic field. The largest moon in the solar system, Ganymede likely has a metallic core that is big enough to generate its own field. It is the only moon in the solar system known to do so. However, recent research indicates that another of Jupiter's moons, Io, may also generate its own magnetic field.

This image shows Ganymede (bottom left) orbiting the giant planet Jupiter.

Did you know...?

Jupiter's magnetic field was discovered by accident. In 1955, astronomers Bernard Burke and Kenneth Franklin were working with a large group of radio antennas at the Carnegie Institution of Washington near Washington, D.C., when they accidentally detected radio waves coming from Jupiter. Later research showed that the radio signals were given off by electrons trapped in a strong magnetic field around the planet.

SATURN, URANUS, AND NEPTUNE

The magnetic field of the giant ringed planet Saturn has a surface-level strength similar to Earth's. As you learned earlier, Earth's geographic poles and magnetic poles are in different spots. However, Saturn's magnetic poles and geographic poles are perfectly aligned—they form one single line.

The magnetic fields of Uranus and Neptune, however, are severely tilted. The north and south magnetic poles of these planets are far from their geographic poles.

A bright aurora lights up the south pole of Saturn. Like the auroras on Earth, Saturn's light show is caused by the interaction of the planet's magnetic field with charged particles carried by solar wind.

WHAT ABOUT MARS AND VENUS?

Scientists have discovered a magnetic field on Mars, but it can be detected only in certain areas on the Red Planet's surface. This leads scientists to believe that Mars is no longer actively generating the field. Instead, the magnetized material in Martian rocks is probably left over from a time when the planet had an active magnetic field billions of years ago. Similar patches of magnetized rock have been found on Earth's Moon, which also lacks an active magnetic field.

Venus is the only planet on which scientists have found no evidence of a magnetic field. Billions of years ago, a magnetic field may have existed on Venus, but the planet now lacks the physical or chemical properties in its core to produce one.

THE SUN'S MAGNETIC FIELD

The Sun has a magnetic field caused by the movement of electrically charged particles in clumps of gas beneath its surface. The magnetic field of the Sun is very complex, with some areas thousands of times stronger than other areas. The strongest spots of magnetism sometimes force huge, visible eruptions of gas called **solar flares** to shoot into space from the Sun's surface.

The magnetic field of the Sun goes through cycles in which its field lines become more distorted and twisted. Sunspots are dark areas where surface temperatures are cooled by intense magnetic activity. When the field lines are most distorted, the number of sunspots reaches a maximum. When the field lines are least distorted, the number of sunspots reaches a minimum. This **sunspot cycle**—from minimum to maximum and back to minimum—lasts about 11 years.

When sunspot activity is at a maximum, the Sun gives off more electromagnetic radiation and electrically charged particles. When the radiation and charged particles get close to Earth, they can disrupt radio communication, disable satellites, and black out electrical power. Sunspot maximums happened in 1989 and 2000. Scientists expect the next maximum to happen in 2011.

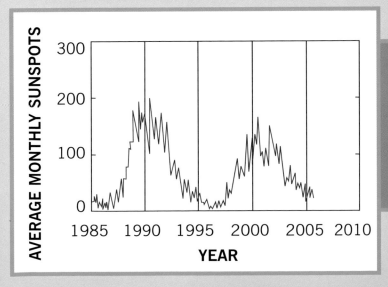

Solar activity peaks roughly every 11 years, as measured by the number of sunspots detected. This graph shows the average number of sunspots per month from 1985 through 2005.

NEUTRON STARS

Most stars are believed to have a magnetic field. The strongest known magnetic fields surround neutron stars—the smallest and densest kind of star. When a large star uses up all its hydrogen and helium fuel, it first collapses and then explodes. The small spinning core left behind is a neutron star. Scientists believe that neutron stars are only about 12 miles (20 kilometers) across—yet they may contain three times as much mass as the Sun. Mass is the amount of matter in an object.

A neutron star has a magnetic field billions of times stronger than any magnet on Earth. This magnetic field generates an electric field that causes charged particles to shoot out from the star's surface. The particles form powerful beams of radio waves, X-rays, or other electromagnetic radiation. As the star rotates on its axis, telescopes detect the beams as a series of pulses, which can be used to study the orbit and properties of the star.

MAGNETARS

Magnetars are neutron stars with super-strong magnetic fields. They produce magnetic fields that are a quadrillion (a thousand trillion) times stronger than the magnetic field of Earth. The magnetic field of such a star is so strong that it causes "starquakes" that pump out bursts of gamma rays into space.

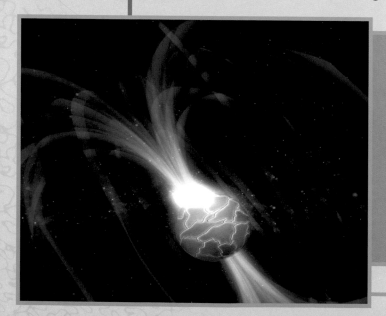

This explosion of light is a magnetar known as Soft Gamma Repeater 1806–20, which produced the brightest flash of light ever detected from beyond our solar system. The image, created by an artist at NASA, shows the magnetar bursting gamma rays into space. The flare of gamma rays was detected in December 2004. It was so powerful that the light bounced off the Moon and lit up Earth's upper atmosphere.

GAMMA RAY BURSTS

Gamma ray bursts are the most powerful known explosions in the universe. They occur when stars collapse or two neutron stars collide. As the stellar material blasts through space, it collides with gas and dust, producing afterglows that last for days or weeks. Computer simulations of such collisions show that they produce magnetic fields that are trillions of times stronger than Earth's.

This drawing of a gamma ray burst shows its awesome power. The force of the explosion creates a light as bright as the rest of the universe combined. Gamma ray bursts appear randomly in the night sky and are thought to be at the very edge of the observable universe.

RECENT DEVELOPMENTS Looking for Gamma Rays

In October 2002, the European Space Agency launched a gamma ray laboratory into space. The International Gamma-Ray Astrophysics Laboratory (INTEGRAL) helps astronomers better understand the forces behind gamma ray bursts, black holes, supernovae, and neutron stars.

Integral's equipment includes a **spectrometer** to measure gamma ray energy and an imager. When gamma rays collide with particles in space, the spectrometer detects, interprets, and records the force of the collision. The imager makes pictures of the objects emitting the gamma rays. Since its launch, Integral has detected gamma ray bursts nearer to Earth and fainter than any others ever recorded.

ELECTROMAGNETISM AND THE BIG BANG

Electromagnetism is one of the four fundamental forces at work in the universe, along with gravity and the weak and strong nuclear forces. Today, each of these forces works separately from the others. However, many scientists suspect that at the moment the universe was created in the Big Bang, all four forces were combined into a single great force.

The forces would have all been combined because of the extremely high temperature, pressure, and energy that existed during and immediately after the Big Bang. As the universe cooled and grew larger, the forces separated.

UNITED FORCES

It might be hard to imagine how electromagnetism could be combined with other forces, but physicists have shown how this can happen. In the 1970s, physicists Sheldon L. Glashow and Steven Weinberg (both of the United States) and Abdus Salam (of Pakistan) developed mathematical formulas showing that the electromagnetic force and the weak nuclear force are two parts of the same force.

Through experiments in a particle accelerator, other scientists later confirmed that these physicists were correct. Experiments showed that when energy levels and temperatures can be made high enough, the electromagnetic force and the weak nuclear force act as a single force.

Further experiments in particle accelerators showed that the strong nuclear force can become impossible to tell apart from the weak nuclear and electromagnetic forces. This happens at even higher energy levels and temperatures. Ideas that unite the different forces are called **grand unification theories.**

Most researchers leave gravity out of grand unification because it is so different from the other three forces, which mainly affect atoms. The effects of gravity are extremely weak on individual atoms. Still, some physicists are working on a "theory of everything" that would explain all four fundamental forces with a single set of mathematical and scientific formulas.

QUESTIONS FOR SCIENTISTS OF TOMORROW

There is much about the Big Bang that scientists do not understand. For example, exactly how and when did the first atoms—and then the first stars and galaxies—form after the Big Bang? How did the universe expand so fast after the Big Bang? And, in a question that may be impossible for scientists to answer, what existed *before* the Big Bang? The answers to the universe's most puzzling questions will not come overnight. But in seeking to unravel these mysteries, unknown discoveries will continue to surprise us.

Centuries ago, people were amazed to find that a magnetic needle could guide a ship. Today, those same magnetic forces lead us in new directions. From the electric motor to the superconducting electromagnet, inventions powered by the forces of magnetism have shaped our modern world. The study and use of magnets and electromagnetism will let us look deeper inside the tiny atom and farther into the cosmos than we ever could before, and ultimately, take us to the very limits of our imagination.

This photo shows the Hubble Ultra Deep Field, the most distant, and oldest, visible light ever seen. The thousands of galaxies shown were the first to appear after the Big Bang. The light from these far-off galaxies began traveling to Earth about 13.7 billion years ago.

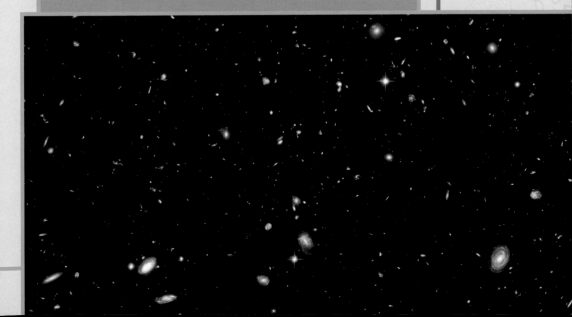

Further Resources

MORE BOOKS TO READ

Gould, Alan, and Stephen Pompea. *Invisible Universe: The Electromagnetic Spectrum from Radio Waves to Gamma Rays.* Berkeley, Calif.: LHS Gems, 2002.

Nankivell-Aston, Sally, and Dorothy Jackson. *Science Experiments with Magnets.* Danbury, Conn.: Franklin Watts, 2000.

Parker, Steve. *Electricity and Magnetism.* New York: Chelsea House, 2005.

USING THE INTERNET

Explore the Internet to find out more about magnets and electromagnetism. You can use a search engine such as kids.yahoo.com and type in keywords such as **magnetic field**, **electromagnetism**, **magnetic levitation**, **electromagnet**, and **electromagnetic radiation**.

These search tips will help you find useful websites more quickly:

- Know exactly what you want to find out about first.

- Use only a few important keywords in a search, putting the most relevant words first.

- Be precise. Only use names of people, places, or things.

Disclaimer
All the Internet addresses (URLs) given in this book were valid at the time of going to press. However, due to the dynamic nature of the Internet, some addresses may have changed, or sites may have changed or ceased to exist since publication. While the authors and publisher regret any inconvenience this may cause readers, no responsibility for any such changes can be accepted by either the authors or the publisher.

Glossary

alloy   material made up of a mixture of metals

alternating current   electric current that changes direction, usually many times per second

amplitude   distance from a peak (high point) or trough (low point) to the midpoint of a wave

armature   rotating part of an electric motor (usually a wire coil wrapped around an iron cylinder) that becomes an electromagnet when an electric current passes through it

atom   smallest complete unit of matter

aurora   streamers or bands of light that appear in the sky at night, especially in polar regions

bow shock   shock wave formed when solar winds collide with Earth's magnetosphere

chlorofluorocarbon (CFC)   gas consisting of chlorine, fluorine, carbon, and hydrogen, believed to cause depletion of the ozone layer

continental drift   theory that the continents broke away from a single landmass and gradually drifted to their present locations

diamagnetic   weakly repelled by a magnetic field

electromagnet   coil of wire wrapped around a magnetic material, such as iron, that produces a magnetic field when an electric current flows through the wire

electromagnetic induction   process of creating an electric current using a changing magnetic field

electromagnetic radiation   waves of energy with electrical and magnetic components caused by disturbances in electromagnetic fields

electromagnetic spectrum   range of different types of electromagnetic radiation, from short-wavelength gamma rays to long-wavelength radio waves

electromagnetism   magnetism produced by an electric current

electron   negatively charged particle in an atom

encoded   converted from sound waves into a code

ferrite magnet   strong type of permanent magnet that has many uses, especially in electronic devices

ferromagnetic   describes a material capable of becoming a permanent magnet, such as iron, nickel, and cobalt

frequency   number of waves that pass a particular point per second

friction   force that opposes the pushes and pulls of other forces

galvanometer   instrument used to detect the strength and direction of an electric current

gauss   unit for measuring the strength of a magnetic field

geomagnetic reversal   when Earth's magnetic field changes direction and the planet's north and south magnetic poles switch places

grand unification theory   theory that attempts to unite the weak nuclear force, the strong nuclear force, and electromagnetism

gravity   force of attraction between all objects

hertz   unit used to measure frequency

hybrid magnet   powerful magnet consisting of a superconducting electromagnet and an ordinary resistive electromagnet

ionize   to give an object an electric charge

irradiation   use of electromagnetic radiation to make chemical or biological changes in material, such as killing bacteria in food

levitate   rise or float

magnetic domain   group of atoms with aligned magnetic fields

magnetic field   area around a magnet where magnetism can be felt

magnetic lines of force   rays of magnetic energy that make up a magnetic field; also known as magnetic field lines

magnetic pole   one of the two poles of a magnet; area where the forces of attraction and repulsion are strongest

magnetism   force in magnetic materials that causes them to attract or repel other objects

magnetite   type of mineral that has strong magnetic properties

magnetometer   instrument that measures the strength and direction of a magnetic field

magnetosphere   region surrounding Earth, or another celestial body, in which charged particles are trapped and directed by that body's magnetic field

magnetotail   portion of the magnetosphere that is pushed away by the Sun

meteorologist   scientist who studies and predicts the weather

nebula   cloud of gas and dust in space

nuclear fusion   process of converting matter into energy by combining the nuclei of atoms

nucleus   central part of an atom

orbits   travels around a larger object in a curving path

paleomagnetism   study of the changes in Earth's magnetic field over time

particle accelerator   device in which atoms and subatomic particles travel at high speeds until they collide and produce new particles

permanent magnet   material that retains its magnetism when not exposed to a magnetic field

plate tectonics   theory that Earth's surface is made up of huge plates that are continually moving

polygraph machine   lie detector

resistance   force that opposes the flow of electricity

resistive magnets   ordinary electromagnets that lose energy as heat when electric current passes through their wire coils

solar flares   visible eruptions of gas that shoot into space from the Sun's surface

solar wind   stream of energetic particles that flows from the Sun

solenoid   coil of wire that acts as a magnet when an electric current passes through it

spectrometer   device that measures gamma ray activity

strong nuclear force   force that holds together all the particles that make up an atom's nucleus

sunspot cycle   amount of time between one period of maximum sunspot activity and another period of maximum sunspot activity, typically about 11 years

superconducting magnets   magnets made of superconducting metals cooled to very low temperatures that do not lose energy as heat while conducting electric current

superconductor   material that conducts electric current at extremely low temperatures without any loss of energy

supernova   exploding star

temporary magnet   material that loses its magnetism when not exposed to a strong magnetic field

tesla   unit for measuring the strength of a magnetic field; equal to 10,000 gauss

transformer   device that increases or decreases the voltage of an electric current

turbine   device that consists of a bladed wheel that is turned by the force of moving water or steam

visible spectrum   wavelengths of the electromagnetic spectrum that can be seen by the human eye

voltage   force behind the flow of electricity

wavelength   distance from the peak (high spot) or trough (low point) of one wave to the same point on the next wave

weak nuclear force   force that plays a part in certain processes by which the nucleus of a radioactive atom decays, or breaks down

Index